KEEPSAKE CRAFTS

BUTTONS

KEEPSAKE CRAFTS

BUTTONS

JO MOODY

SUNSET PUBLISHING CORPORATION
MENLO PARK, CALIFORNIA

A QUARTO BOOK

First Printing January 1995

Copyright © 1995 Quarto Inc.
Published by Sunset Publishing Corporation,
Menlo Park, CA 94025

ISBN 0-376-04257-5

Library of Congress Catalog Card Number:
94-068057

For more information on Keepsake Crafts
Buttons or any other Sunset Book,
call 1-800-634-3095.

This book was designed and produced by
Quarto Inc.
The Old Brewery
6 Blundell Street
London N7 9BH

Senior editor Sally MacEachern
Editors Geraldine Christy, Jane Royston
Senior art editor Amanda Bakhtiar
Designer Nick Clark
Photographers Paul Forrester, Chas Wilder
Illustrator Elsa Godfrey
Art director Moira Clinch
Editorial director Sophie Collins

Typeset by Poole Typesetting, Bournemouth
Manufactured in Hong Kong by Regent
Publishing Services Ltd
Printed in China by
Leefung-Asco Printers Ltd

CONTENTS

INTRODUCTION

There is an amazing variety of buttons to be found in every shape, size, and color imaginable, made from many different materials including wood, horn, glass, plastic, metal, and shell. They can be plain, molded into fun shapes or carved with intricate designs, and you can even make your own.

Many people have collections of beautiful buttons, but all too often they sit unseen and unappreciated at the bottom of a box. The projects in this book will inspire you to use those buttons not merely as fastenings on clothes, but in the most innovative ways. Antique and contemporary buttons make wonderful jewelry, for instance, and add decoration to all kinds of fashion and home accessories. The only limit to what you can do is your imagination!

SHELL BUTTONS

Shell buttons (above) have a beautiful glossy sheen. Markings can be strong and pronounced or very subtle, and the "wrong" side often looks as attractive as the right side.

NOVELTY BUTTONS

Novelty buttons (below) make ideal decoration on both children's and adults' accessories. Animals and alphabet letters used to spell out words are great fun for children's clothes.

BUTTON TYPES

There are two basic types of buttons. A shank button has a loop on the wrong side, which can be molded from the same material, as shown here, or made of metal. Sew-through buttons can have any number of holes, but two or four are most common today.

PLASTIC BUTTONS

Plastic buttons (left and right) can be dyed any color, and molded or faceted to resemble metal, glass, ivory, or almost any other material. They are much lighter and less expensive than the real thing.

METAL
BUTTONS
Buttons
made of a
base steel with a
gold or silver finish
offer endless possibilities for
decoration. Bright, polished buttons in
geometric shapes create a modern look, while
intricate, antique-style buttons are perfect for jewelry and
accessories.

COVERED
BUTTONS
Metal or plastic button molds
are available in many sizes (above). They
can be covered with fab-
ric either to match or
contrast with the base
fabric for a perfect fin-
ishing touch. Fabric can
also be embroidered before
being used to cover a button.

WOODEN
BUTTONS
Wooden
buttons (right) can
be plain, polished to
show off the natural
grain, carved, or colored
with attractive designs. They are light-
weight and can be used on all kinds of fabric.

HORN AND LEATHER BUTTONS
Horn buttons look wonderful when highly
polished to show off their markings or
carved with intricate designs. Leather
buttons with contrasting stitching give a
natural feel to heavy knitwear.

FIMO® BUTTONS
Marbled and millefleur buttons (see
p.10–11) are simple to make from Fimo®
or similar modeling materials, and offer
endless design and color possibilities.

RHINESTONE
BUTTONS
These glamorous buttons (above) are perfect for creating a glitzy evening look on
clothes and accessories. They look particularly dramatic on a black or dark background, as they sparkle and catch the light.

MATERIALS

Most of the projects in this book require little in the way of special equipment, although there are a few items that you will find helpful. If you do not already have these in your sewing or household tool box, they are inexpensive to buy and are readily available from notions departments, craft outlets, and by mail order.

Having the correct equipment at hand will make working on the projects much easier and will also give a professional finish, so it is worth investing in the right tools before you start. Shown here are the basic items you will need.

FINDINGS

Findings are the metal components used in jewelry making, although some are decorative enough for other purposes.
1 Jump rings link various jewelry components and findings. **2** Triangle bails are used to hang thicker buttons, which will not take a jump ring. **3** Eye pins are threaded through buttons to link them together and to other findings. **4** Head pins are used in the same way as eye pins. **5** Barrel clasps consist of two halves which screw together. **6** Pierced earwires come in various shapes. **7** Bell caps conceal multistrand thread ends on a necklace or earrings. **8** Pin backs provide a base for sewn or glued buttons. **9** Posts with butterfly fastenings for pierced ears. **10** Decorative clasps. **11** Screw and clip fastenings for unpierced ears.

PLIERS

Small jeweler's pliers with fine, smooth tips are needed for working with findings, and are used to bend head and eye pins into shape, make loops, open and close jump rings, and fix crimps. If they do not have a cutting edge, wirecutters will also be needed.

AWL

An awl is used for starting holes in leather prior to stitching on buttons.

NEEDLES

The type and size of needle required will depend on the buttons (especially the size of the hole) and the materials and techniques being used.

1 Beading needles are ideal for fine fabrics. **2** Quilting needles are fine enough to go through most buttons and fabrics. **3** Leather needles, with their sharp, angled points, are useful for stitching buttons onto belts or bags. **4** Curved needles are extremely useful for decorating unusual ready-made objects such as hair accessories and bags.

THREADS

Your choice of thread will depend on the size of buttons and the technique being used.

1. Invisible thread is ideal for fine work, as are silk and cotton threads. **2** Nylon line has great strength and is useful for jewelry making and more unusual items such as button people (see pages 62–3). **3** Bright cotton threads can be chosen to match a color scheme. **4** Metallic and iridescent threads add interest.

GLUES

Your choice of adhesive will depend on the materials you are using. Check the manufacturer's instructions before application.

1 Two-part epoxy glue is very strong and usually dries to a clear finish. **2** A good, general-purpose white or yellow craft glue will suffice for most projects.

SCISSORS

Good scissors are essential for working with buttons.

1 General-purpose craft scissors. **2** Small, sharp-pointed embroidery scissors are used for snipping thread ends.

MAKING YOUR OWN BUTTONS

Making your own buttons is easy and fun, and will give you the extra satisfaction of knowing that you have made a whole project yourself from start to finish. Fimo® modeling clay is inexpensive and is available in a wide choice of colors, making your options for button design almost limitless.

The finished buttons are baked in the oven to create a durable finish that is suitable for a variety of purposes, including jewelry, clothing, and hair accessories. Bear in mind, however, that these buttons are not washable and would therefore be unsuitable for an item that is likely to need frequent washing (unless you remove the buttons first).

fabric, do so at this stage so that you know where to position the stitching.

2 Run a gathering thread around the fabric edge and place the button at the center. Pull the thread up so that the fabric is stretched tight across the button.

3 Snap the back of the mold onto the wrong side to hold the fabric securely.

MARBLED BUTTONS

I Knead two or three colors of Fimo® modeling clay until soft and roll them into equal log shapes. Twist them together (left). Continue to knead and twist the clay colors together until you achieve the marbled effect (right). Take care not to over-knead the clay, or the colors will blend together and you will lose the effect.

COVERED BUTTONS

I Using a compass, draw a circle of a larger circumference than the button mold, and cut it out. If you wish to embroider the around the spiral as shown. Re-roll the clay gently to maintain the shape.

MILLEFLEUR BUTTONS

1 To make the design shown here, take Fimo® modeling clay in dark blue, green, medium blue, red, and yellow (or the colors of your choice), warm them, and then knead them until soft. Roll out thin squares of dark blue and green clay, place them together and then roll them up to make a spiral design.

3 Roll out a thin piece of dark blue clay, and roll it around the inner colors, keeping it as even as possible. Roll out the finished log more thinly.

2 Roll out the marbled clay evenly and cut it into slices using a sharp craft knife.

2 Roll out a thin log of red, and roll a thin layer of medium blue evenly around it. Cut the logs into several lengths. Make similar lengths of yellow clay, and, alternating this with the blue-and-red roll, position them

4 Cut the log into slices with a sharp craft knife and mold them into the button shapes of your choice. Form the holes with a toothpick or wooden skewer, and bake the buttons in the oven following the manufacturer's instructions.

If you wish, paint or spray the buttons with a light, even coat of varnish to complete.

3 Make holes in the buttons with toothpicks or wooden skewers, and bake them in the oven following the manufacturer's instructions.

If you wish, paint or spray a light, even coat of varnish over the buttons and let them dry thoroughly.

JAZZY JACKET

Spice up a plain but bright-colored jacket by adding more color with a novel button trim. Stunning contrasts work well together, giving the jacket a totally new look.

Rows of colorful buttons on the pockets, with larger buttons on the cuffs, give this plain blue jacket a really stylish finish.

Italian designers are renowned for producing clothes with both style and humor, and it was their inspired use of buttons as decoration on clothes that influenced this jacket. You can use buttons in lots of unusual ways to add designer detail and to make a more eye-catching feature of an ordinary element. Necklines can be enhanced, while hems and waistbands can be emphasized by outlining them with attractive buttons in harmonizing or clashing colors. Collars, cuffs, and pockets can be given the same treatment – cover them lavishly with buttons for a really ornate finish, or just dot with buttons for a more understated look.

Brightly colored buttons have been used to decorate the pocket tops and cuffs on this jacket. Using one bold color on top of another bold color usually requires some courage, but the result can be sensational, as you can see here. The buttons look good enough to eat, like bright-colored candy, and add a brilliant jazzy finish. For those who prefer a less striking design, simply swapping the original buttons for more colorful ones will add some individual flair.

The buttons can have shank or hole fittings and need to be sewn in place overlapping each other to cover the area completely. If you decorate the pocket tops of a jacket, be sure to sew the buttons securely, as they will get quite a lot of wear from hands going in and out frequently.

A plain tuxedo comes to life with the help of some strategically placed rhinestone buttons. These add wonderful light-catching sparkles and contrast beautifully with the black fabric. Other buttons could be substituted for a different look – gold or bright colors would be very effective.

Having scoured used clothing shops, thrift stores, and various bazaars and markets, I discovered this classic tuxedo at a yard sale. The suit was a real find at a bargain price. It was in good condition and, after dry cleaning, looked brand new. Many people throw out amazingly good clothes, and it is easy to become addicted to searching for original pieces to customize.

This jacket was given a more feminine feel by decorating the silky satin lapels with an assortment of rhinestone and modern clear plastic buttons to add glamor, while still retaining the sleek, stylish, tailored look. The jacket originally fastened with a traditional *passementerie* braided button which was the worse for wear, so this was replaced with a single spectacular rhinestone button to complete the sophisticated look.

A more understated effect can be achieved by simply swapping the original fastening buttons and those on the cuffs for more elaborate or opulent ones. You could add further interest by decorating the breast pocket and perhaps the side pockets with additional buttons. The rhinestone buttons used here add sparkle, but pretty mother-of-pearl buttons, with their lustrous sheen, or antique silver or gold buttons, would look just as stunning.

On this jacket, the buttons on the lapels were sewn in place individually with a beading needle and a fine invisible thread of the type often used for machine embroidery. A single strand of silk embroidery thread in a matching color could also be used. The important point is to cause as little damage as possible to the fabric, in case you decide one day to revert to the original look.

SPARKLING TUX

Glittering rhinestone buttons add jazz and pizzazz to a second hand tuxedo, turning it into a designer-style original that is perfect for glamorous evenings out.

NATURAL WINNER

Vests are extraordinarily versatile items of clothing – they can be sharp and tailored, casual and unstructured, or dressy and elegant, and look as good worn with a business suit as they do with jeans.

A perennial fashion favorite, the vest has come a long way from its traditional roots – the simple tailored version worn under a suit jacket has been banished to the city and has made way for a more colorful cousin. A vest can be dressed up or down to suit the occasion and the character of its owner, turning it into an accessory rather than just an item of clothing.

Inspired by attractive but expensive designs available in stores, this vest was made from a loose-weave raw silk using a simple dressmaking pattern. The soft beige fabric harmonized beauti-fully with a set of horn buttons that I had in my collection; but some wooden buttons and others which had a natural feel also complemented the material particularly well. I decided to use all the buttons to create a totally original and eye-catching vest with a fashionable natural theme.

In this instance, the vest was finished, so the buttons had to be added afterward. The tricky part is sewing them to the top fabric only, so that unattractive stitching does not show through on the lining, which would prevent the garment from being worn open. You may find it easier to partially complete the vest, attaching the lining only at the front edges before adding the button decoration. The lining will

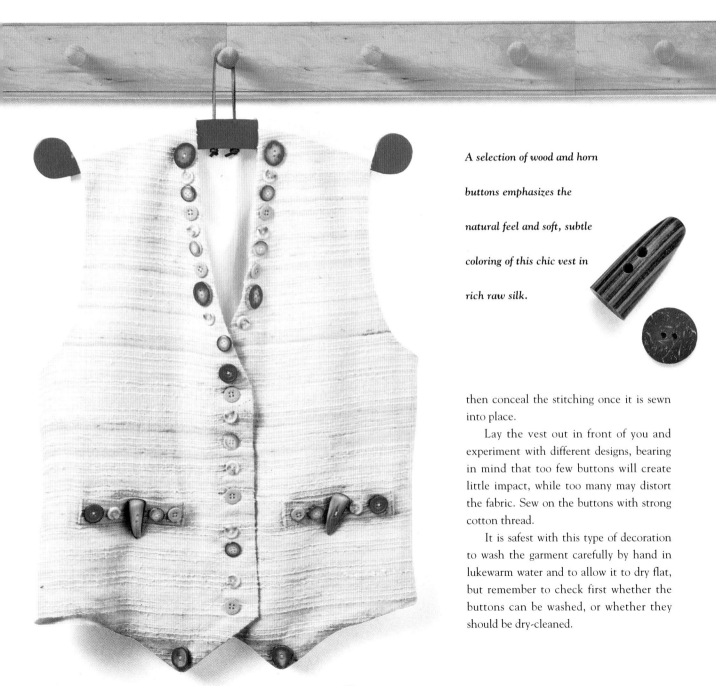

A selection of wood and horn buttons emphasizes the natural feel and soft, subtle coloring of this chic vest in rich raw silk.

then conceal the stitching once it is sewn into place.

Lay the vest out in front of you and experiment with different designs, bearing in mind that too few buttons will create little impact, while too many may distort the fabric. Sew on the buttons with strong cotton thread.

It is safest with this type of decoration to wash the garment carefully by hand in lukewarm water and to allow it to dry flat, but remember to check first whether the buttons can be washed, or whether they should be dry-cleaned.

A solid-colored vest can be transformed with the help of an eye-catching button design. For a special occasion, light, bright buttons look particularly effective on black fabric.

PRECIOUS PEARLS

This plain black vest has been decorated with small mother-of-pearl buttons clustered in stylized floral motifs, each of which is high-lighted with delicate seed pearls.

Plain black fabric can be decorated in many ways to create totally different looks. Mother-of-pearl buttons and seed pearls were used here, but small gold buttons and *rocaille* beads could also be incorporated into this or a similar design for a more ornate and dressy finish.

This simple vest was made using a basic paper pattern. First cut out all the pieces from the vest fabric and lining material, and then lay out the two front pieces. Remembering to allow for the seams, place the buttons on the front pieces and experiment with different patterns and designs until you have decided exactly what you want. Mark the position of all the buttons with tailor's chalk, and sew them in place before attaching the front pieces to the lining (in this way, the unattractive stitching on the wrong side will be concealed inside the lining). If you wish to update a vest that you already have in your wardrobe, as in the previous project, be sure to make tiny, neat stitches to prevent an unattractive finish that would show if the vest were worn unbuttoned.

Complete the vest, following the instructions on the pattern, and then wear your finished design with pride in the knowledge that it is unique and original.

Square and round buttons in

varying sizes highlight the cable

pattern on this hand-

made sweater. The

tassels, which

were simply

made from

three bead

strings thread-

ed in place

under the but-

ton, add the perfect

finishing touch.

SILVER HIGHLIGHTS

see how they look. Let the design and pattern on the sweater guide you, and try to highlight any interesting detail. If you are decorating a plain stockinette-stitch sweater, be brave and dot buttons all over it. Choose buttons of a suitable weight for the type of garment – big, heavy, metal buttons look best on chunky yarn, while mother-of-pearl or glass buttons are ideal for finer yarns.

Once you have decided on the design, sketch it on paper and then, following this guide, sew on each button individually using strong thread in a color to match the garment.

Give a favorite sweater a bright new look by personalizing it with decorative buttons. Choose interesting shapes and textures to add designer flair, or bright, clashing colors for a fun look.

Buttons can be added as decoration to both purchased and hand-knitted sweaters. Use the buttons as simple trims around collars, cuffs, and welts, or to accentuate the texture, as in this example.

Choose colors to coordinate or to add richness. Wood and horn buttons go well with cream or tweedy Aran knits, for instance. The luster of shell buttons enhances almost any garment, as do precious metals, especially those with antiqued finishes. Primary colors in bold shapes provide dramatic contrast to plain black or dark fabric such as navy or bottle green.

Lay the sweater out flat and experiment, placing buttons here and there to

The finished sweater will need to be washed with care by hand and dried flat, or dry-cleaned (refer to the recommendation on the yarn label if the sweater is hand-knitted, or to the manufacturer's instructions if it is a ready-made item). Be sure to bear the aftercare in mind when selecting your buttons, as this will affect your choice.

Classic shoes can be cleverly updated with simple button

decoration. Whether you choose antique

buttons to add a classy, expensive touch, or

witty buttons for sheer fun, they can transform

a plain pair of shoes into

something extra special.

FANCY
FOOTWORK

Two antique-style buttons sewn to the fronts of the dressy shoes

below create an instant designer feel. Rhinestone buttons could be

similarly placed

for elegant

evening shoes.

Glued all over a basic pair of heels like large polka dots, the white buttons below really come into their own.

These fun, watch-design buttons, with the addition of some old necklace chain, make a pair of shoes witty and stylish.

Buttons are incredibly versatile, and they come in such a wonderful array of colors, shapes, and sizes that they shouldn't have to be confined to functional uses on clothes. With a little ingenuity and artistic license, you can create your own unique high-fashion footwear to step out in style.

The beauty of shoe decoration is that it does not always involve lots of buttons, nor do they need to be a matching set. One or two buttons strategically placed can make an ordinary pair of shoes look exclusive, as the shoes opposite show. These buttons had shank fittings and were sewn on using a curved needle and strong button thread.

The large white buttons on the shoes in the middle were rather uninspiring and unattractive on a jacket, but created a chic and much-admired pair of shoes. Make sure

that shoes are completely clean and free of dust before gluing on the buttons, and use a waterproof adhesive.

I snapped up the "watch" buttons shown above on sight, as I hadn't seen anything like them before. These had shank fittings, and I attached the chain with the aid of pliers and jump rings (used for making jewelry – see pages 8–9) to the shanks before sewing the buttons in place. This was a perfect way in which to display an awkward number of buttons.

This type of decoration on shoes is fine for occasional wear, but will not stand up to a lot of heavy use – however, nor will some of the most expensive shoes that you can buy at the shoe store!

Give last season's hat a brand new look by using buttons to add style and humor. Be bold and daring or subtle and understated with your design, and create an original head-turning accessory!

HAT TRICKS

Buttons sewn to hat bands can create a variety of effects. Natural-colored buttons complement the "pot" hat above perfectly, and wood and horn buttons suit the felt hat on the right.

A few buttons and a little imagination can transform a very ordinary hat into a trend-setter with designer flair. You could cover the whole crown lavishly with buttons, creating a real conversation piece, or, if you feel less adventurous, you could simply highlight the brim or band.

Choose the buttons to complement the style of the hat, as well as the occasion. It is a good idea to baste the buttons in place on one thread to check the design first, before sewing each in their final position. Use strong thread in a matching color.

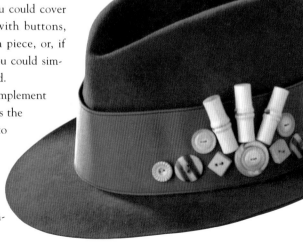

The striking flower buttons decorating the band on the cream straw hat below add a lovely summery feel that would be perfect for a wedding or christening, or even a day at the races. Sportier felt hats, such as the one shown below left, can be trimmed with wood and horn buttons in natural colors, with the buttons positioned on one side of the band in place of a more traditional feather or flower decoration.

The brown felt "pot" hat on the right makes an ideal candidate for fun decoration – buttons can be sewn all around the rim, or even all over the crown, as shown here. The buttons on this hat have been sewn randomly, but you could sew them in patterns for a more structured look.

The crown of the "pot" hat above has been covered in a delightful assortment of quirky buttons collected over a period of time. They are of all shapes and sizes, and add a touch that is both stylish and humorous. On the other "pot" hat, on the opposite page, wood, leather, and horn buttons have been used with the occasional golden highlight to decorate the brim and set off the dark brown background beautifully.

You can have a lot of fun with button decoration on hats and could even decorate interchangeable bands to give the same hat a totally different look to suit both your mood and the occasion. Just let your imagination run wild and create your own totally original accessories.

BUTTONED UP

Creative use of a jumbled collection of buttons can jazz up an uninteresting purse, giving it a designer look for little cost. Choosing a unified color scheme adds a little flair.

A button trim can cleverly disguise a tired-looking purse and give it a fresh new look. You can also transform a bargain handbag quickly and easily, and no one will know that it hasn't cost a lot. Select buttons that will suit the shape and color of the purse, and turn it into an exciting accessory. Rhinestone buttons add sparkle and are perfect for creating a glittery evening look, while gold, silver, and bronze buttons have an enriching effect, evoking the style of a bygone era. Be careful with polished finishes, as these can look too brassy and tend to stand out unless

Pearl buttons turn this basic evening purse into an elegant accessory.

A red-and-gold color scheme was chosen here to set off the navy and create a bold but sophisticated look. Strong contrasts of this kind can be extremely effective. The gold in some of the buttons adds a rich touch of luxury and matches the strap fastenings to give the bag a ready-made feel.

they are surrounded by similar buttons. Grouped together, however, they really do look stunning, and bright young designers frequently use them for impact.

Your chosen design can be classy and understated, with the buttons sprinkled at random over the surface like gemstones, or bold and strong to inject a sense of humor. Strong primary colors can add a striking contrast to a plain background, as well as a little fun, brightening up the most ordinary and uninspiring of purses.

On the purses shown here, the buttons were stitched to the gussets on each side, overlapping each other to cover the area completely. Fabric and synthetic-leather bags are the easiest to decorate in this way, using basic sewing techniques. Be sure to use a fairly strong thread and to attach the buttons securely, as the bag may be subjected to a reasonable amount of wear and tear as it is carried around. It is best to stitch buttons in place on fine leather using a special leatherworker's needle with a fine point. With thick hides, you may need to use an awl (see page 8) to make holes before stitching the buttons in position.

TASTEFULLY TRIMMED

The ingenious use of buttons for trimming and decoration can refresh the most jaded or out-of-date clothes and accessories, giving them a whole new lease on life.

Revamp an old leather belt with interesting button detail. Groups of buttons have been put together to create this simple design.

The fringed trim on this sweater was created by threading buttons together to make a long "necklace." The buttons chosen were of different shapes and sizes, but were all made of wood, horn, and leather to create a natural effect which complements the beige color of the sweater.

You will need to work with two threads to hold the buttons in place. Start one thread by bringing it up through a hole in the first button, then put it down through the hole in the next button, and so on. The second thread runs parallel to the first but is worked the other way – that is, down through the first hole, up through the second hole, and so on. Leaving a small gap between each button, thread on as many as you require for the length, alternating the styles and shapes along the "necklace." Knot each end. Next, cut smaller lengths of string: you will need one piece for each gap between buttons. Fold each length in half and tie it over the two threads between each button as you would a gift tag – push the looped end under the threads, and then bring the other two ends up over the two threads and pull the ends through the loop. Knot to secure. Trim the fringe and knot wooden beads to the end of each "tassel" to finish.

To decorate a belt such as the

The neckline of this plain V-neck sweater is enhanced with buttons made of wood, horn, and leather. String emphasizes the "natural" effect and echoes the stitching on the leather buttons, setting off the rich brown color scheme perfectly.

one shown on the left, the buttons can be glued in place, but, for a more durable finish, it is wise to stitch them in place. When decorating a thick leather belt, you may need to use an awl (see page 8) to start each hole. Plan the design first, and then sew each button in place using a strong thread and a special leather needle.

Quite spectacular effects can be achieved by using lots of buttons with one underlying color theme to accentuate an unusual accessory. The gold stripe on this classic tie was used as the inspiration, and the tie was then decorated liberally with lots of gold buttons in all shapes and sizes to create an imaginative effect. The tie could be worn in the conventional way, or slipped through the belt loops on a pair of evening slacks or a skirt and tied loosely for a casual look.

Sew the buttons in place, using fine invisible thread and

ALL TIED UP

Take one basic tie, decorate it with a large assortment of gold buttons, and you

have a brand new look that will add dash to your wardrobe and a little humor to

any social occasion.

This striped tie is lavishly

decorated with a variety of

gold buttons. A good start-

ing point is to select a color

from the design on the tie,

or from the

tiny stitches. The buttons can be sewn randomly all over the tie, as in the design shown here, or you could position them more uniformly, perhaps using just a few in one area to create a focal point. The intended purpose of the tie will obviously influence the placing of the but-

background, and to

use this as

tons to some extent, so bear this in mind when you are planning your design. Choose rich metallic finishes and jewel-like colors for evenings, and bright primary colors or wooden buttons for day.

Use this idea to

the basis

for your button

color theme.

inspire you to create original accessories that you can be sure no one else will be wearing. Have fun playing around with different ideas and designs and experimenting with colors and patterns until you come up with something really effective. There are lots of other acces-sories which can be given the same treatment, such as scarves, stoles, hats, gloves, evening purses, and shoes, and there are more ideas for some of these throughout the book. You will soon realize that the possibilities are endless, and you will find yourself looking for different and unusual buttons every-where you go.

ELEGANT EARRINGS

Beautiful buttons can be transformed into unique jewelry designs that will draw admiring comments. Use

these ideas for earrings to inspire you to start looking through your button box.

The lovely earrings

shown here are just

some of the many

designs which can

be created with a

few buttons and a

little imagination.

They are all

deceptively simple

and quick to make.

Earrings are some of the easiest and most effective items to decorate with buttons, whether they are simple studs or ornate drops. Button jewelry is also an original way of using up odd buttons or displaying those too precious to use on clothing. Try combining antique or modern buttons to produce truly innovative pieces.

The simplest designs are easily made by gluing earring findings (either clips or posts and butterflies (see page 8)) to the backs of a pair of attractive buttons, such as the crested blazer buttons with shank fastenings shown below. More interesting effects can be achieved by linking two buttons together with fine wire or glue. Small buttons with shanks can be wired to larger, hole-fastening buttons to create

pretty stud earrings, or small beads can be strung and attached so that they cascade from the central holes.

Use simple silver hoop earrings as a base, and decorate each of them with two crystal buttons to make a glamorous pair of earrings for evening. Create elegant drop earrings by linking the shanks of small gold buttons with jump rings to form loops, and then hang these from the shanks of larger buttons before adding the findings.

A glance through the selection of jewelry findings available will fire your imagination, and, once you get started, you will find yourself thinking up a wealth of designs. Have fun experimenting with and linking different shapes, sizes, and colors of buttons in a variety of ways, and create your own unique collection of jewelry that will be the envy of your friends.

Buttons can be used to trim many different hair accessories,

giving them a unique personal stamp or simply transforming them from practical

daytime to more sophisticated evening wear.

HAIR
DRESSING

Faux tortoiseshell slides and combs are particularly attractive when combined with shell or pearl buttons. Padded black velvet or satin hairbands look glamorous with sparkling rhinestone and metallic buttons for evening wear. You could even continue the theme on other accessories to go with your outfit, such as a purse or shoes – refer to other projects in the book for ideas.

To make your own head-turning accessories, you need to experiment and plan your designs before securing the buttons. This is not always easy on narrow, curved surfaces, but double-sided tape is perfect for holding the buttons in place temporarily while you work out the design.

When it comes to sewing, you may find a curved needle useful to deal with any awkward angles. You can use thread to add some texture to the design by sewing on the but-

tons with fine ribbon or raffia, for example, or you can simply choose a matching color or use invisible thread.

For gluing, it is essential to use a glue that is suitable for the materials with which you are working, and to make sure that both surfaces are free of dust and grease. Wiping the surfaces with a lint-free cloth dipped in turpentine is one way of doing this. You may need to roughen the surfaces of some plastic materials slightly with sandpaper before gluing – this will provide better adhesion and good contact.

Buttons make wonderful additions to all kinds of hair accessories, from combs to hairbands. Choose harmonizing or contrasting button colors to suit your outfit and your mood.

Bold gold and black buttons on a velvet band make a stunning bracelet. This could be complemented by matching earrings or even a choker necklace.

BROOCH
& BRACELET

Button jewelry is really easy to make and produces truly original and individual pieces. No two designs will be the same, especially if you use antique buttons.

It is possible to make attractive jewelry from just a small assortment of buttons by using a little imagination and ingenuity. The bracelet shown opposite was made with a mixture of antique and modern buttons to create a beautiful finished piece. To start the design, choose one or two buttons that you really like and create a color scheme around them. Once you begin to see the possibilities, you will soon become addicted to searching out button stores in every place that you visit! Antique fairs, yard sales, and bazaars are other great sources for old buttons. Search through the clothes for interesting and unusual designs which could be cut off and used for decorative purposes.

The buttons for this bracelet were sewn onto an elasticized velvet band to create a chunky evening effect with a designer feel. The buttons were overlapped so that they covered the band completely for a really rich, ornate look.

The button brooch on this page was inspired by a wonderful seashell button which, along with the mother-of-pearl and starfish buttons, created a seashore theme. Filmy ribbon conceals the cardboard base and gives a seaweed effect that ties in with the rest of the design. Scattered small gold beads create the impression of sand.

Let the buttons do the inspiring. Few people who become interested in buttons can resist building up a large collection, and you will find that once you have spotted one or two buttons on a particular theme, you will start discovering them everywhere. Then you will find exactly the right button to work into a design, setting it off perfectly and creating a really dazzling piece of jewelry.

This delicate seashore brooch looks very intricate, but it is extremely easy to make. The mother-of-pearl button provides a perfect foil to the bright gold shell and starfish.

The buttons of this
unusual neck cowl are
enclosed in small
"pockets" of machine-
knitted nylon monofila-
ment, although fine net
would work as well.

NECK & NECK

There is a stunning variety of

buttons available which look too good

just to use in the traditional way and

which can be made into fabulously

original jewelry.

Choose buttons to suit your design. Some of the wonderfully glamorous buttons on this necklace have glass-jewel stones which glisten under the light, and the burnished seashell buttons add an ornate, antique feel.

The buttons have shank fittings and were threaded on a length of jewelry wire with small gold beads interspersed to accentuate the rich effect.

The button decoration was worked in three sections – two identical side pieces and the center drop – which were then sewn onto gold cord using invisible thread. To make each side section, take a piece of wire a little

Rich gold

cord provides the

base for this splendid

necklace, which would look

stunning worn with a simple black dress.

more than twice the length required and thread on the buttons and beads. To prevent the buttons from dropping forward, fold the wire in half and thread this end back along the length, through the beads and looping over the button shanks. Use jewelry pliers (see page 8) to turn the end of the wire through the shank of the last button to finish it off neatly. Bind each shank tightly to the cord with invisible thread, hiding the thread among the beads and taking it through the cord every now and then to secure it. Leave a small gap at the center front for the drop. Make this section in the same way, but turn the ends of the wire into a loop and then sew it to the cord.

The beautiful neck cowl opposite is a wonderful way of using up odd buttons. Translucent fabrics, such as this nylon monofilament, can create a particularly delicate effect for evenings.

Colorful novelty buttons enhanced

with embroidered stems make this

plain white child's shirt

really attractive. Buttons can be used

this way on almost any item of clothing.

The easiest way to give clothes a brighter look is to replace boring and uninspiring buttons with fun novelty versions. These are now available in all shapes and sizes and in fabulous bright colors that kids will love. Most are designed especially for children's clothing, so they should be both safe and washable, but check first if you are in any doubt.

SUNFLOWER SHIRT

Bright and shiny novelty buttons are a great way of personalizing children's clothes. Ordinary garments can be turned into

desirable designer-like originals with very little time and effort.

With a little imagination, you can make an item really special by using buttons to create a design your child will love. You can see on the shirt shown here that these sunny flower buttons look great with stylized stems and embroidered leaves to highlight the effect. Sewing the buttons onto the pocket and collar and adding two ladybug buttons continues the theme.

Use the buttons to inspire added detail. Ducks and boats can have wavy lines embroidered underneath them to look like the ripples on a pond, for example, and simple stars can be made to look like shooting stars with a few small beads or stitches. There are all kinds of possibili-

ties, and if you check out the novelty buttons in good notions departments, you are sure to find inspiration and come up with lots of your own unique and fun ideas.

Fruit-shaped buttons are easy to find and can be used to create a fruit-bowl motif on a pocket, with different fruits used for the buttons and on the collar. Alphabet buttons are also widely available and are fun when combined to spell out names, while numbers can be used to create a clock face on casual wear such as sweatshirts. Add a little humor to a school shirt or jacket with buttons in the shapes of pencils and pencil sharpeners.

DIZZY DINOSAURS

All children love dinosaurs, and these bold-colored buttons are just the thing to

brighten up a little boy's suspenders and gloves and

make them fun to wear.

Novelty buttons of popular characters are a great way of jazzing up a child's favorite outfit. Let children choose the buttons in the shapes of well-loved characters or animals, and then use them to give a lift and add a little humor to simple accessories such as gloves or hats, bags, hairbands, scarves, and even drab school backpacks.

These tartan-plaid suspenders and tomato-red gloves have been given a new look with bold tyrannosaurus and stegosaurus buttons in bright blue and red. You can simply use the buttons on their own, arranging them to make an attractive

Bright blue dinosaur buttons on children's gloves are

enhanced by a basic embroidery design in white yarn. The

stitches used include couching, French knots, and stem stitch.

design, or add bright embroidered details to continue the theme of the buttons, as on this cheerful pair of gloves.

Making your own buttons is also great fun, and, with polymer-modeling clays such as Fimo®, it couldn't be easier. See pages 10–11 for tips and techniques, and use the wide range of colors available to produce your own bold, attractive designs.

Button-making is also a good project in which to involve children, giving them the chance to create their own original works of art. Attaching the buttons that they have made could even be their first sewing lesson if they are old enough, and if an adult keeps a watchful eye.

Depending on the design, buttons can be sewn on at random or used in groups to create motifs. A complete picture could be worked on the back of a sweatshirt using lots of different buttons to make a real conversation piece at a party.

Let your imagination and your children's ideas run wild, and really have fun customizing their wardrobes.

This pair of plaid suspenders is transformed with a few bright buttons. Blue and red have been used here to match the plaid, but any other bright colors would look equally effective.

As with boys' clothes, fun buttons in the shapes of well-loved

characters or animals are a great way of dressing up a little girl's accessories and adding

a personal touch.

ALL THINGS NICE

Novelty buttons are available in such a wide spectrum of colors and shapes that you might find yourself overwhelmed. Select buttons in coordinating shades to suit a particular outfit, or pick out vibrant, clashing colors to create a really eye-catching impact. Where most children are concerned, the brighter the buttons you use, the more they will love them!

Pink is by tradition a little girl's favorite color, and this often does seem to be the case. It was the color chosen to decorate this simple headband, and it works well on the navy background. This particular little girl is crazy about animals, so I selected cats and ducks as her main characters, and added hearts and a sassy ladybug to complete the design. They were stitched securely on each side of the bow, with

allowances made for the "stretch" factor in wear. Be careful not to use too many buttons, as they may catch in the hair when the band is put on and taken off, and could also be uncomfortable when worn all day.

Lots of other little girls' accessories also make good candidates for button decoration, including belts, gloves, shoes, and bags. Fabric bags are the easiest type to decorate, but a leather needle with its special point (see page 9) will make short work of tough vinyl and hide.

Along with all the other projects for children in this book, it is essential that the decoration is anchored in place securely. Most novelty buttons are fairly small, so it is very important that little fingers cannot pull off the buttons and put them in a child's mouth.

Pink and white animal buttons stand out beautifully on a navy headband. This type of elasticized band is widely available and is also easy to make.

This shoulder bag is given a summery feel with butterflies and strawberries decorating the front flap and a couple of ladybugs adding a final touch. Matching buttons on summer sandals would also look pretty.

Buttons can be used in lots of ways on throw pillows – create a colorful trim

with tiny buttons, or use them as part of an overall design.

ALL
SQUARE

The clever addition of decorative buttons can give worn throw pillows a bright new look and makes a refreshing change from the trims traditionally used. Experiment with different patterns, laying out the buttons on the empty cover to see the effect before stitching them in place.

Choose buttons to suit your décor. They do not necessarily have to be a matching set in an antique or contemporary style, but remember that,

Flat buttons sewn through the pillow pad

create an upholstered effect

(right); a trim of pearl buttons on

velvet, with a self-covered button in

the middle, makes an elegant pillow

(center); and bright gold buttons of different

shapes gleam on cream taffeta (far right).

unless the pillow is used purely for show, buttons can be quite uncomfortable to lean on. Bearing in mind this comfort factor, it is best to opt for fine, flat buttons which won't dig into the back.

An alternative is to give the pillow an upholstered look by stitching the buttons through the pad, as on the one shown on the left. This creates a more interesting effect, as well as making the pillow more comfortable to lean on. Position the buttons in place on the front of the cover, then stitch them in the normal way, but take the thread through to the back of the inner pad, pulling it tightly to create a dent in the surface. You can sew buttons in the same position on the other side of the cover at the same time.

The beautiful pearly finish of shell buttons decorating a pillow complements any room, especially a well-lit one where the luster will catch the light. The small buttons used to trim the pillow in the middle create a really luxurious effect on the rich velvet background. Four triangles of fabric make up the top of this pillow, with a self-covered button (see page 10) sewn through the pad in the center.

On the right-hand example, pale taffeta provides the perfect foil to flat gold buttons. The large square buttons have been sewn through the pad, with the smaller buttons stitched to the surface only.

It is wise to choose washable or dry-cleanable buttons for throw pillows; otherwise, you will have to remove them when the cover needs cleaning.

A pretty button and

rings of colored felt

make an attractive

variation of the

upholstered

cushion on the far left.

Patchwork combines

beautifully with buttons

to give a "homey"

feel. The buttons

on this cover

were sewn

through all the layers to

create a traditional

quilted effect.

Patchwork, one of the oldest of home crafts, uses scraps of fabrics cut into shapes to form a pattern. These are then sewn together to form a whole piece of fabric with a mosaic effect, which can range from subtle and understated to really bold and bright. Many different pattern shapes are used in traditional patchwork designs, but one of the simplest is based on the square, as used here. This straightforward pattern is perfect for the beginner, provided that each square is cut to exactly the same measurement. You will find templates for the pattern shapes at most good craft outlets, and using them

The craft of patchwork is traditionally used to create pretty bed covers,

pillows and many other attractive items. This charming and simple-to-make quilt

illustrates how effective the combination of patchwork and buttons can be.

QUILTED TREASURE

cutting the fabric into identical, regular shapes a much simpler task.

This delightful cover was made from a pretty patchwork of coordinated fabrics in bright fresh colors, ingeniously trimmed with buttons to create the quilted effect. Join the squares together to make a patchwork fabric that is the required size for your project. When you have finished it, join it to the backing fabric, with polyester batting "sandwiched" between the two layers. Stitch all the layers together and sew bias binding around the edges to finish them.

To complete the cover, sew buttons to the points at which the corners of the squares meet, sewing through the batting

and pulling the thread tight to create the quilted effect. As a decorative twist on the cover shown, stranded embroidery floss in a contrasting color was sewn through each button and tied, leaving long, wispy ends. You can make a small knot in each of the ends to prevent the floss from fraying and working loose.

The finished cover is charming and would look good on any child's bed. It is, however, important to point out that it is not advisable to decorate babies' crib covers with button trims, just in case the buttons were pulled off and swallowed. The cover should be washed carefully by hand.

Interior décor can be updated and given designer detail with the clever use of unusual buttons. These terrific tiebacks add subtle glamor and style to the simplest curtains, without looking overdone.

TERRIFIC TIEBACKS

Buttons can be used effectively in many interesting ways, adding an individual artistic touch to a variety of items. Once you begin to let your imagination run wild, you will come up with all sorts of original ideas to enhance your home.

The texture of the corded tieback in soft, subtle colors sets off the pearly sheen on this collection of shell and mother-of-pearl buttons for attractive tiebacks which complement the fabric of the curtains. It is also a unique way of putting a collection of beautiful buttons permanently on show and is sure to be a real conversation starter.

The buttons can be sewn on to cover the cord completely, or to form a focal point. You could also decorate fabric tiebacks in the same way to create an equally interesting effect. Choose buttons in colors to coordinate with the room for a harmonious look, but go for striking contrasts of color if you wish to create a really dramatic impact.

The buttons on this corded tieback were sewn in position using a cream stranded embroidery floss. Working with three strands together, take the thread through the center of the cord and bring it out at the point at which the next button is to be secured. The finished tieback can be topped with an ornate tassel.

There are many other accessories for the home which can be given an interesting new look with some simple button decoration – just let your imagination run free and don't be afraid to be inventive.

Buttons in subtle,

natural shades

sewn onto corded

tiebacks give an

elegant feel to these

pale blue curtains.

An elaborate tassel

adds the perfect

finishing touch.

HOT SPOTS

Bring a dash of fun and a splash of color to a child's room

by cleverly trimming a variety of accessories with bold but-

tons in bright, sizzling hues.

Imaginative use of buttons in exciting color combinations can achieve spectacular results. Once you begin, you will find that even the most ordinary objects can be given a fresh new look using the simplest decoration, as shown here. Toy boxes and other accessories can be revamped with buttons glued on as decoration, but be sure to use a tough epoxy adhesive so that inquisitive little fingers can't remove them.

The buttons on this lampshade and curtain look like a spattering of bright-colored candy or polka dots. The pattern on the curtain was worked out roughly first, and the position of the buttons marked with tailor's chalk. They were then sewn on in the traditional way to make them as secure and as child-proof as possible. If you are using buttons with shanks, choose a thread in a color to match the fabric, but

buttons with central holes can be sewn with brightly colored contrasting thread to add extra zest to the finished appearance.

The same design was used with great success on the lampshade. Here, the buttons were made to look as if they were sewn in place, but they were in fact glued. Take a bright contrasting thread through the holes several times and knot it securely on the wrong side; then use a strong, heat-resistant craft adhesive to glue the buttons firmly in position.

The beauty of these ideas is that, when the children get bored with the design, or grow out of it, the accessories can easily be replaced at little cost. Unpick the thread carefully and remove the buttons from the curtains and lampshade when you feel like a change, and re-use them for some of the other projects shown in this book!

The bright primary

colors of these buttons

really sing out against

the rich cobalt-blue

background of the

curtain and would

make a perfect corner

for a child's bedroom.

This romantic work of art was inspired by the Victorian era and

is made up of a collection of old buttons, a couple of pieces of lace collected on my travels, and a treasured card.

PRETTY AS A PICTURE

These lovely buttons lay unused and unappreciated at the bottom of a needlework box. I discovered the lace in Amsterdam in a store selling bric-à-brac and thought that it was too precious to use on something frivolous, while the card, from a special friend, could not be discarded, yet had no practical use. Displayed together, they make a most enchanting picture of mementoes and treasures that would otherwise gather dust.

Having chosen your frame, you need to figure the size of your picture. Cut out a piece of craft interfacing to fit inside the frame exactly; then cut a piece of fabric 2 inches wider than this. Fold the fabric over the interfacing and stitch to secure it in place, making sure that the stitches don't show through on the right side. Arrange your treasures on the fabric, and stitch or glue them in place. Mark the position of the card with tailor's chalk, and then stitch on the lace with invisible thread. The buttons for this picture were sewn on individually using embroidery silk, but, if you have a collection of antique buttons still on their original cards, they can look attractive displayed in groups and glued in place complete with the backing card. Use a clear-drying adhesive that is suitable for fabric both for the keepsake card and the buttons. Let the picture dry completely, press it carefully if necessary, and then place it in the picture frame and secure.

Treasure samplers such as this one make wonderful personalized gifts, especially as bridal or new-baby presents.

CREATIVE CARDS

Interesting buttons can be used to make individual greeting cards with truly personal messages of good wishes and in different styles to suit every possible occasion.

Blank cards are available in a variety of sizes and colors. They are perfect foundations for making your own personalized greeting cards. Decorate them with brightly colored novelty buttons to welcome a new baby, to wish someone a happy birthday, or just to say hello. You can draw extra detail on the front of the blank cards to complement the button design, and the borders become especially effective when

This small card made with white duck buttons on a navy background is simple but very effective, and could be used for any festive occasion.

Bright, primary-colored buttons resemble polka dot wrapping paper on the embroidered present and would enhance any Christmas or birthday greeting.

fabrics can also be used to set off the pattern of the buttons. Work out the button design before stitching the embroidery design, marking the position of each button with tailor's chalk. Use stranded silk or cotton embroidery floss to embroider words to suit the occasion, using cross stitch or a mix of stitches, if preferred. There are many books and magazines available with charts of alphabets and borders which will inspire and help you. When the embroidery is complete, sew the buttons securely in place and mount the fabric inside the blank card, gluing it securely.

Pastel-colored shell buttons make a pretty design on this circular blank card. You can buy blank cards in many different shapes and sizes to suit all your design ideas.

highlighted with gold or silver marker pens.

There is such a wonderful choice of novelty buttons on the market that you will never be lacking for inspiration for creating cards suitable for any occasion. Flower buttons are available in a range of shapes and sizes and could be worked into small bouquets and even placed as an arrangement in a vase. The only limit to what you can do is your imagination!

If you sew the buttons onto Aida (an embroidery cloth which comes in a variety of colors), you can work details and words in embroidery stitches, although other

Some delightful buttons in the shapes of buggies inspired these new-baby cards, and the tiny toys completed the theme. These could also be used to make charming birthday cards for small children.

It may be difficult to believe, but the delightful trinket boxes shown opposite started

out life as containers for cheese similar to those below. A little creativity has

transformed them and concealed their humble origins.

BOXING CLEVER

Traditional French cheese boxes are often made from plywood and are far too good to throw away. Decorated with buttons and braid, they can take a new lease on life and make exceptionally charming little boxes to give as gifts, or to keep on your own dresser or desk.

Any selection of buttons can be used. If you have only a few buttons, the design can be worked as a simple decorative

motif or border; but the boxes do look especially attractive with their lids completely covered with an extravagant assortment of buttons.

Lightly sand the wood first and then apply a coat of antique-pine varnish to deepen the color. Glue braid around the side of the box to hide any writing before adding the button decoration.

Varnish will enrich and enhance the wood, but different effects can be

Empty cheese boxes

in square or round

shapes make ideal

items for button

decoration and are

just the right size

to sit nicely on a

dresser.

These

pretty trinket boxes

really look like

expensive purchased

items, but couldn't

be easier

to make.

achieved by painting the surfaces with acrylic paints. Cover with a primer such as white latex first, and then paint on the color of your choice. Gold and silver are always attractive, and jet black can give the effect of Japanese lacquer. You could also try using decorative paint techniques such as marbling or faux verdigris and découpage around the side of an otherwise plain box.

Work out your design before gluing the buttons in place. Buttons with shank fittings will not sit easily on the top of the box while you do this, but double-sided tape will keep them in place temporarily. Make sure that the surfaces are clean and free from dust to create a good contact

(you may also need to roughen the surfaces slightly with an emery board to create better adhesion). Use a clear-drying, strong adhesive when covering a box totally, overlapping the buttons and letting them support each other. Let the box sit for at least 36 hours to make sure that the buttons have set firmly.

The lids here have

been covered with

antique-pine

varnish to deepen

the color, but you

could use acrylic

paint or even fabric

to cover the surfaces

before adding the

buttons.

Why not try mounting favorite photos in attractive frames

of your own design? Creative button decoration can turn even the simplest,

plainest frame into a work of art.

IT'S A FRAME-UP

Picture frames look

very effective either

highlighted with or

entirely covered by

buttons. These

inexpensive frames

have been complete-

ly transformed using

simple button

decoration.

Polished, mirror-finish gold buttons in bold geometric shapes give a modern look to the inexpensive frame on the far left. The buttons were placed around the frame and juggled until the final design was decided, and then glued in place. Use a strong glue – a clear-drying one is best, as any excess won't spoil the design. If the glue spills out through the holes in the buttons, carefully remove it when it dries. Both surfaces should be clean and free of dust and grease to provide a good contact. Test one button first, letting it dry completely for 36 hours. If it breaks away from the frame with little force, you may need to roughen the surface of the frame slightly with an emery board to create better adhesion for the glue before gluing on the other buttons.

The old-gold buttons and pickled-pine frame in the center look as if they were made for each other. The buttons had

shank fittings and were tricky to glue in place, so they were used to highlight the frame detail and positioned in the corners. One side of the shank was glued to the side of the frame.

Matte-gold highlights added extra interest to the shell, mother-of-pearl, and pastel buttons covering the right-hand fabric frame. The buttons were sewn using a curved needle threaded with stranded embroidery floss. Using three strands, secure the thread under a button where it won't be seen. Take the needle up through a hole, across the button and down through the other hole, bringing it up through the fabric at the position of the next button. Continue sewing on the buttons, overlapping them until the frame is completely covered. When you reach the end of the thread, make a secure knot and conceal it under a button.

BUTTON PEOPLE

Make these charming little people by simply stringing

buttons together to form the bodies, arms,

and legs. Add a bead to create the head, and top it with a

button for a hat.

These cheerful

button people will

brighten up any

corner of your

home. Make five or

six and turn them

into a mobile for a

child's room, or use

them as novel

decorative

ornaments for a

Christmas tree.

String your chosen buttons on invisible nylon thread or matching cotton thread. Use buttons with different-sized hole fittings – the smallest for the arms, medium-sized ones for the legs, and the largest for the body. Buttons with shanks are ideal for the hands and feet, or you could attach bells to add a jolly jingle. The number of buttons required will depend on the sizes used.

Cut two lengths of thread, each approximately 18 inches long. Fold one length in half, and push one end through a bell or the shank of a small button. Now take one end of the thread through one hole of a medium button and the other end of the same thread through the second hole. Thread on several more buttons of the same size to form a leg. Make the other leg in the same way.

Next, take both ends of thread from one leg, and push them both through one hole in a large button to start the body. Take the two threads from the other leg through the second hole of the button. String on as many buttons as required to complete the body.

When the body is the correct size, separate the threads on one side and take just one of the pair through one hole in the smallest buttons to make an arm. When this is the right length, take the thread through the shank of a button to make the hand, and then take it back up through the holes on the other side. Repeat this for the other arm.

You can now add a button to make a neck if required, or simply take all four ends of thread through a hole pierced centrally in a large bead or small styrofoam ball to make the head. Knot the thread tightly, as close to the head as possible, to secure it. Trim the thread and add a dot of glue to anchor the knot. Tie colored or invisible thread to a final button to hang up the button person, and glue it onto the head to make a hat.

Give your button people individual characters by selecting buttons to suit – create a clown with bright primary colors, for example, or a jolly sailor in classic navy and white.

ACKNOWLEDGMENTS

The author would like to thank the following people for their help and support while putting this book together. First, Linda Collins and Terry Meinrath at Button Treasures who kindly supplied the majority of the wonderful buttons used to create the projects; Lesley Stanfield for her stylish designs; Lynn Galliver, Jackie Shou, and Sandy Darby for their sewing skills, which were greatly appreciated; and last but not least my family, especially my mother and sister without whom the book would not have been completed.

Quarto would like to thank Button Treasures, 4 Charterhouse Buildings, Goswell Road, London EC1 for supplying the majority of the buttons used in this book.

Quarto would also like to thank the craftspeople who supplied projects for the book: Susie Freeman 38; Helen Milosavljevich 42; Lesley Stanfield 24–5, 28, 32–3, 48–9; Janet Slingsby 36–7, 40; Lesley Tonge 46. All other projects were made by Jo Moody.

Finally, Quarto would like to thank the models: Laura Bangert, Clara Chan, Giulia Hetherington, Laura Wickenden, and Willoughby Werner.